GOD'S GIFT WITHIN

The Story of the Joshua Quilt

by Gail Howard Gibson

Interviewed by Marylee MacDonald

GOD S GIFT WITHIN: THE STORY OF THE JOSHUA QUILT.
Copyright © 2018 by Gail Howard Gibson
Published by Marylee MacDonald
Tempe, AZ 85282
www.maryleemacdonaldauthor.com

Design by Bob Ryan
wix.com/bobryan/portfolio1

Photography by Christiaan Blok
www.cblok.com

All rights reserved. Printed in the United States of America. No part of this publication may be reproduced, distributed or transmitted in any form or by any means, including photocopying, recording, digital scanning, or other electronic or mechanical methods, without the prior written permission of the publisher, except in the case of brief quotations embedded in critical reviews and certain other noncommercial uses permitted by copyright law. For permission requests, please contact Marylee MacDonald.

PUBLISHER'S CATALOGING-IN-PUBLICATION DATA

Gibson, Gail Howard (Roberta Gail Howard), 1955- | Macdonald, Marylee, interviewer.
God's gift within: the story of the joshua quilt/by Gail Howard Gibson; interviewed by Marylee MacDonald.
Story of the Joshua quilt.
Tempe, AZ: Marylee MacDonald, [2018]
ISBN: 978-0-9962503-7-5 (hardcover) | 978-0-9962503-5-1 (ebook) | 978-0-9962503-6-8 (audiobook) | 978-0-9962503-9-9 (Kindle)
LCSH: Christian life. | Bible--Study and teaching. | Patchwork quilts--Religious aspects-- Christianity. | Quilting--Psychological aspects. | Bible. Joshua--Illustrations. | Bible. Joshua-- Inspiration. | Life change events--Religious aspects--Christianity. | Stress (Psychology)-- Religious aspects--Christianity. | Adjustment (Psychology)--Religious aspects --Christianity. | Inspiration--Religious aspects--Christianity. | Caregivers--Religious aspects--Christianity. | Self-actualization (Psychology)--Religious aspects--Christianity. | BISAC: CRAFTS & HOBBIES / Patchwork. | RELIGION / Christian Life / Inspirational. | SELF-HELP / Motivational & Inspirational
LCC: BV4510.3 .G53 2018 | DDC: 248.4--dc23

To all the women who taught me to sew, to my mom who lived the most Godly life of anyone I have ever known, and to my husband and soul mate for supporting me and giving me a lifetime of adventures.

―――――――――――――― & ――――――――――――――

Out of your relationship with God
come life's greatest treasures
—fellowship, wisdom,
peacefulness of soul,
eternal hope,
gladness of heart,
direction and meaning,
and a glorious purpose in all you do.
—*Roy Lessin*

Table of Contents

A Special Note	ix
Gail Howard Gibson, Your #1 Quilting and Bible Study Expert	1
Getting Started With Quilting and Bible Study	4
Life's Obstacles Present Opportunities	7
Finding Community After a Move	9
Her First Major Breakthrough With Quilting and Bible Study	11
Quilts and the Holy Spirit	13
Designs Inspired by Scripture	19
The Bible Study That Inspired The Joshua Quilt	23
Interpreting the Book of Joshua in Fabric	28
Overcoming the Obstacle of a Cross-Country Move	31
Examining the Quilt Square By Square	35
Standing Back From the Quilt	53
Prairie Points Represent the 70 Elders	56
Meeting The Theologian	59
How The Worlds of Quilting and Bible Study Have Changed	63
Disruptive Events Turn Out To Be God's Greatest Gifts	65
How Readers Can Discover Their Own Gifts	69
Quilting and Time Management	72
Overcoming Obstacles	74
About Marylee MacDonald	78
Contact Gail Howard Gibson	79

ALSO BY MARYLEE MACDONALD

Bonds of Love & Blood
Montpelier Tomorrow

A Special Note

———————————— & ————————————

Dear Reader,

Thank you for claiming your copy of *God's Gift Within: The Story of The Joshua Quilt*. I'm guessing that you're an ordinary person, struggling with the unexpected events life throws our way.

In this book I will share the skills, tools, and techniques I discovered while making a quilt based on the Book of Joshua. I hope these "life lessons" will strike a chord with readers who value family, faith, and creativity.

This book was originally created as a live interview with my friend and fellow author Marylee MacDonald.

That's why it reads as a conversation rather than a traditional "book" that talks "at" you. I wanted you to feel as though I am talking "with" you, much like a close friend or relative.

I felt that creating the material this way would make it easier for you to grasp the topics and put them to use quickly, rather than wading through hundreds of pages.

So relax, and get ready to take your quilting and Bible study to the next level. By sharing my journey, I hope to help others stop being afraid of life's challenges, and, with God's help, do what He wants you to do.

Let's get started with how God orchestrated the details in my life and helped me make The Joshua Quilt.

Sincerely,
Gail Howard Gibson

Photos by Christiaan Blok

Gail Howard Gibson, Your #1 Quilting and Bible Study Expert

Marylee:
Hi everyone and welcome to *God's Gift Within: The Story of The Joshua Quilt*, an interview with Gail Howard Gibson. My name is Marylee MacDonald, and today I'm talking with quilting and Bible study expert Gail Howard Gibson, about how God orchestrated the details in her life to help her make The Joshua Quilt. Welcome, Gail Howard Gibson.

Gail Howard Gibson has been a quilter and active in her faith community for over 50 years. She's graciously consented to this interview to share her experiences so that ordinary people struggling with life's unexpected events can stop being afraid, and with God's help discover their own unique gifts.

Gail Howard Gibson, thank you again for joining me in this live interview. Let's just jump right in so you can share how you got started and what our audience can learn and apply when it comes to quilting and Bible study.

My first set of questions is about your background and experience in the field of quilting and Bible study so that people of faith, quilters, Bible study groups, storytellers, caregivers, and quilt museum curators in our audience can understand who you are, where you're coming from, and how you got started. Then we'll jump into your thoughts about what you would do if you had to start all over again when it comes to quilting and Bible study so our audience can understand how they can apply what you've learned to their own lives.

Could you tell us a little about yourself in terms of background, education, and experience in quilting and Bible study?

Gail:
Well, thank you for having me today. I grew up in a small town in Georgia. Both parents worked, and I had a mentally disabled older brother. Apart from that I had pretty much a normal childhood.

My mom was one of those people that, even though she worked, she would come home in the evenings and she always had to have something to do with her hands. She was oftentimes either crocheting or sewing. She always said that idle hands were the devil's workshop. I had a mentor—an example—in my life of someone who was always making good use of their time and doing something for others.

As I grew up I went to junior high, and I had the opportunity to study home economics in the seventh and eighth grades. It was an unusual opportunity because normally you would have had to take a PE class, and you wouldn't have had home economics until you really got into high school.

That was one of my first experiences with sewing. It opened up kind of a partnership with my mom. My mom would try to show me how to sew. I was at that age where I thought I knew more than she did, even though she was an expert. Our first attempt at sewing would be Barbie doll clothes, which were just extremely hard to make.

Then, while I was in the midst of taking this home economics class, I decided to be an overachiever and try to make a three-arm-hole, wrap-around dress. This is one time I will say my mother really helped me out. She was not a parent who would do the project for you, but in that particular case, she really did help me out.

As I continued my education I went on into high school, and I again took a home economics class. Then when I went to college I decided, at first, that I was going to be an accountant, and then I realized that no, that really wasn't what I wanted to be. I ended up majoring in home economics, and graduated with a general home economics degree with minors in business and interior design.

During that time when I was at Berry College, I took tailoring classes. Not just tailoring but also making draperies. I learned quite a lot of technique in college, and I continued to sew just on my own, whether I was making something to wear or making something that was decorative. I never really did too much with quilting up until that point.

Getting Started With Quilting and Bible Study

———————— & ————————

Marylee:
When did you get started quilting?

Gail:
Well, my mom retired, so to speak, from a job, and I had an aunt who quilted all the time. My mom decided to go and help her, and she learned the art of hand quilting. Mother was a perfectionist. She did everything by hand. She cut everything with scissors, not a rotary cutter like people use today. All of her piecing was perfect—every corner met, every point met—but she really wasn't very good at putting color combinations together.

    Mother and I worked as a design team. She would cut these pieces and then she would say to me, "Just pick out two or three squares and put those together."

    She cut, she sewed, she quilted, and I basically just said, "Oh, let's put that square there and let's put that one there." We did this for years. It was only when my daughter was in high school that I decided that I wanted to make quilts for people my mom didn't know. Oftentimes the quilts Mom and I worked on, we both knew who the recipient was. I kind of began to feel like, "Well, that's not really fair to ask her to make quilts for people she doesn't even know," so I started quilting on my own. The first quilt that I really made and gave to somebody was to a young girl. I had served as her mentor in confirmation.

The Story of the Joshua Quilt

Mom and Aunt Gladys

I wanted to make a quilt for her and I made a raggedy flannel quilt. That began me making other raggedy quilts for friends of our daughter's and other family friends' children as they graduated from high school. It was their high school gift. That was the beginning of my true quilting.

Marylee:
What about with Bible study?

Gail:
Bible study has pretty much always been a part of my life. Growing up in a Southern Baptist church, we went to Sunday School, we went to Training Union, and we attended Vacation Bible School. I was a part of the G.A.s, otherwise known as Girls' Auxiliary. At an early age Bible study was a part of my life.

As I got to be an adult and married, there were times when my husband and I moved around, and we did not have a church or Bible study group, but I still read the Bible on a pretty regular basis.

Then at different points in time, I attended Disciple Bible Study, which is a four year program. I also attended B.S.F., the Bible Study Fellowship. Then for a number of years, I was part of a Bible study within my neighborhood.

Marylee:
Has a church community always been important to you or have there been times when you couldn't find one?

Gail:
Church community was always important. I think part of that was because I grew up in a church community. The church we attended was part of the neighborhood. Oftentimes people walked to church. It was kind of a central part of the community.

When I married and began to travel across the United States, my husband and I sometimes found it difficult to find a church that we fit into. When you travel and you live in different parts of the country, you realize that you're not in Kansas anymore.

I couldn't find a church several times that was something that I was familiar with, or that I wanted to be a part of, or that I even felt like that I was welcome to be there when I went. Yes, it has sometimes been difficult to find a church.

Life's Obstacles Present Opportunities

Marylee:
You and your husband raised two children, moved 12 times in 30 years and were caregivers for your mother for 14 of those years. What roadblocks and obstacles did these life events cause, and what blessings came out of those obstacles?

Gail:
Well, if you look at moving as a stress indicator, a cross-country move is pretty high on the list. You're giving all your belongings to someone, they're putting them in a truck, and you don't really know them. They're moving them, in our case, 3,000 miles across the country.

When you get there there's not necessarily always a welcoming committee there to welcome you. Sometimes your belongings make it, and sometimes they don't. Then you have to go through the process of trying to figure out did I really keep that or did I go ahead and give something away? Do I have all my belongings?

That was, I want to say, not just an obstacle, but almost a roadblock. When you consider that you're going to move more than once in your life, and if you have bad experiences moving, it makes you think twice about, "Do I really want to give up what I've got right now and move on to something else?" It's also hard when you have lived for 20 or 30 years in the same place to uproot and leave everything familiar, whether it's your dentist, your hairdresser, your church family, or your friends.

What I would say is that blessings came out of some of these obstacles. The moves opened my mind and my life up to seeing how people in other parts of the United States live. There's different customs. Everybody doesn't go home and eat fried chicken with the family on Sunday after church.

Also, there were times when I would be trying to get a job and employers weren't willing to hire me. They wanted somebody who'd be there for a long time.

I came away thinking, "Well, why not just give the best that you have while you're there?" Why couldn't these people see that I would have been a great employee? Maybe they gave the job to a person who'd been in that community for years and years. But what if some life-changing event happened, and that person didn't get to stay in that position for 30 years? It made me think differently about moving, and that's a blessing because you need to sometimes think differently.

Finding Community After a Move

Marylee:
In your various moves, did you have anyone who helped you settle into a new community or did you have to figure it out all on your own?

Gail:
Sometimes there were people. Really and truly, when I look back at it, there was always somebody.

The first move I ended up 3,000 miles away from home. My husband was in the military at the time. Just shortly after we made a cross-country move, he was deployed onto a tour of duty, and I was not able to go with him. I really didn't know anybody, and yet the people who lived next door to us became friends I could depend on if I needed something. They served a great purpose in my life at that particular point in time.

There was also an incident where, at that same time my husband was leaving the country and in one of his meetings, he happened to run into a former college friend. He hadn't seen him since they had become commissioned, and he really didn't know what had happened to him. As they left the meeting that day, my husband told this guy, "I'm leaving and I'd like you to look out for my wife." He said, "Okay." He was married and shortly after my husband left, he contacted me. Come to find out, his

God's Gift Within

wife and I were born and raised within probably 30 minutes of each other.

God provided those people for me and for us. They took care of me while my husband was gone. When he came back we worried that the three of us didn't know how he was going to fit into the group. He really fit in pretty well, and to this day—and it's been 30 something years ago—we are still friends with those people, even though we do not live close to them. We still keep up with them through Christmas cards, through Facebook, and through e-mail.

Literally with each move there was somebody God provided, and that person said, "Here. Here's flowers."

The very first morning that we'd moved into a new home, I woke up and found flowers on my porch from a neighbor. Another time there was a neighbor down the street. I ran into her only because she was out walking her dog, but from that day on we continue to be friends, and we go to lunch every Friday.

I didn't always have to figure it out on my own. I had to figure out sometimes where the dentist was or maybe go through two or three rounds of trying to find a dentist, but there was always somebody there that God provided.

Her First Major Breakthrough With Quilting and Bible Study

Marylee:
Let's get back to quilting for a second. What was your first major breakthrough with quilting and Bible study?

Gail:
I'd have to say that the first major breakthrough was when I was in Tuscaloosa, Alabama. I was part of the Presbyterian Women of the First Presbyterian Church in Tuscaloosa. The church put out a call to provide 12-inch, quilted squares. These would be given to the global partners attending the third Churchwide Gathering of Presbyterian Women in Louisville, Kentucky. This was a big conference, and it was going to be attended by people from all over the world. They had a theme that was called "God will do wonders among you."

    I decided I would answer the call. I ended up reproducing the conference logo. It was a round circle that looked like a mosaic with a dove descending on it. I reproduced that using the computer and printing it along with verses that I had chosen from John 14:25-27 to make a 12-inch square. At the time I just thought, "Oh well, there'll be a lot of people that will participate in this." It turned out that there were only two other quilters.

At the time I had never even heard of the gathering of Presbyterian women. I ended up finding out later that there were approximately 2400 women attending that conference. Usually when I make something for someone I know the recipient, but this was one of those times I did not know the recipient. To this day I don't know who received that particular square.

Quilts and the Holy Spirit

Marylee:
That's a great story, Gail. You put yourself out there! So, how did creating The Joshua Quilt cause you to step outside your comfort zone?

Gail:
Creating The Joshua Quilt was not something that I had planned on. At the time my husband was possibly considering making another move with his job. My mother was in her 90s and had had some issues with her health. Our daughter was about 700 miles away from home, going to college, and our son was at home—an 18 year old trying to decide what he was going to do with his life, where he was going to go to college, that sort of thing. To take on the responsibility of making a quilt—I didn't have a pattern for it; I would be designing all of it—I was way out of my comfort zone.

Marylee:
Is there one particular story or example you'd like to share that really sums up your experiences in the quilting and Bible study world?

Gail:
Yes. I'm going to go back to talking about being in junior high and learning how to sew, the time I was

taking this home economics class. The thing that's significant about junior high is that it was the first time in my life I had moved. I moved with my parents across town. It doesn't seem like a big deal, but it was because all the friends I'd gone to elementary school with would go to a different junior high school. Here I was across town, and I didn't know anybody, and I had to go to a new junior high and make new friends.

It was somewhat of a scary process at that point in a young person's life. When I went into that junior high, I ended up coming out with three of my very best friends, and really I'm still in touch with all three of them—some closer to me than others, but still in touch. One of these people was a girl who would end up going off to college and marrying a guy from Iowa. She would leave her comfort zone of Georgia and go live out on a farm in Iowa and raise four children. The youngest of her children would be a young woman who, in 2008, would find herself married, expecting her first child, and in the midst of summer flooding in Cedar Rapids, Iowa.

At the time I saw the news, I thought of my friend and knew that her daughter lived in Cedar Rapids, and so I called my friend and said, "How's your daughter? How's your son-in-law?"

She said, "Well, they were completely flooded out, and we had just moments to be able to go over there get some of the things out of their house, some meat out of their freezer, maybe the wedding photos, but just not a lot of stuff, really."

I asked her how could my husband and I help

them. I was expecting to maybe write a check for helping them buy new things for their kitchen or something.

She said, "Oh, no. They have insurance, and they're going to be fine." Then she said her daughter lost her quilt. It was her only quilt.

I had been thinking while we had been talking, "Maybe they need a quilt." I said, "So does your daughter still like purple?"

She said, "Yes."

I said, "What about her husband? What's his favorite color?"

She said, "Blue."

I said, "Okay." I said, "I'm going to make them a quilt," and I said, "It may take me a year, but I'm going to make them a quilt."

You have to understand, when I make a quilt I don't just necessarily go out, buy a pattern, look on the back of it, find exactly how much fabric it calls for, and follow the pattern directions. I pretty much take either a basic quilt pattern or technique that I know and then just be creative with it. The other thing is, I don't make a quilt unless I am really led by the Holy Spirit to make that quilt. My husband has referred to this as quilting for God.

In this particular instance, I took my mom because we were living in Tuscaloosa, and by this point in time she was in a wheelchair, but we went to a fabric store there. I remember I bought almost every piece of fabric that I would use or think about using for this quilt. I must've bought, I don't know, 20, maybe 30 different pieces of fabric. Some of it "fat quarters" (a measure of fabric 18"x 21"), some of it yardage, but just all kinds of blues, and yellows, and purples.

There were umbrellas printed on the fabric. There were raindrops on the fabric. There were things that if you were thinking about a flood, yeah, water would cross your mind.

I decided that I'd make this quilt by a pattern known as The Yellow Brick Road. In each block of The Yellow Brick Road, there are five pieces. This quilt ended up being 90 blocks, so it was a really big quilt.

I only saw my friend one time during this process and talked to her about what I was doing. She was excited and said, Oh, yeah, her daughter and son-in-law would really love this.

Normally, my mom would hand-quilt everything she made, but this was a big quilt, and I wasn't about to ask my mom to hand-quilt it. I took the quilt to the woman who machine-quilts my quilts, and she quilted an all-over pattern of water puddles.

I picked it up—probably mid-November—and it dawned on me my friend and her husband, and maybe part of their family, might be traveling to Georgia to celebrate Christmas, and so I contacted my friend. Sure enough, they were going to be in Georgia, so I had between mid-November and Christmas to put the binding on this quilt, and finish it, and get it ready to take over to Atlanta.

On the day that I took it, I had our daughter with me and we drove over to Atlanta. We were just going to go visit my friend. That was what my friend's family knew. No one else knew that this quilt was a part of the visit or the real reason for the visit. Oftentimes my friend and I had gotten back together. If both of us were down in the Deep South at Christmastime, we made it a point to try to touch base with each other, so it wasn't unusual for us to get together at Christmastime.

The other thing, whenever I make a quilt, I pray about the people who are receiving it. I pray it will be a blessing for them and that it will mean something to them. I also write a letter at the end of completing every quilt. Sometimes I include pictures (if I've taken them along the way) as to how that quilt was made; but mostly I write to them and tell them what my thought process was.

I sometimes give them instructions along the lines of, "Use this. Respect the quilt, but use it. It's machine washable and dryable." I had written a letter to my friend's daughter and her husband, and explained that, "Yeah, I only do make quilts when led by the Holy Spirit."

I told them what the pattern was and I told them how I had picked out these fabrics just for them. Even told them that when our son saw this quilt-top laying out on the floor, he looked at it, and said, "Oh, it looks like Easter."

I thought, "Oh, that's perfect because Easter is a time of new beginnings." I told them in their letter that there had been many a prayer stitched into the quilt, and that I had prayed for them many times, and asked that God would bless them. Anyway, I closed off my little letter to them with the hope that they might feel God's love as they snuggled in under these covers.

When I actually got there and gave them the picture and the quilt, they were just looking at it in awe. By this time, their little girl was able to walk, and she was walking all over it. She loved that quilt. Anyway, I looked at it, and I knew that it had hit its mark and that I had done what I felt like the Holy Spirit had been leading me to. That these fabrics with the umbrellas and the raindrops, that it wasn't a negative necessarily in their life, but a reminder of some event that had happened in their life.

Then weeks or months later I was talking to my friend and she shared what her daughter had to say about this quilt. She said, "I can't believe someone would do that for us, and every time I use this quilt, I think of how God works."

The Story of the Joshua Quilt

Designs Inspired by Scripture

Marylee:
Wow. Wonderful. You originally started off thinking about The Joshua Quilt. Would you like to talk a little bit about making The Joshua Quilt? If someone wanted to make a quilt like that, or a quilt that relates to the Bible, should they start with the Bible or the fabric?

Gail:
I think you should start on your knees and pray, pray, pray. I just think you've got to be in tune with what the Holy Spirit's saying to you in your life right

Little Nova enjoying the Cedar Rapids quilt

then. Maybe there is some Bible verse that continues to just speak to you, and you want to somehow express that in a fabric/textile/quilted piece of work, or sometimes it's just a fabric.

Nowadays people print all kinds of things on fabric. You can buy Bible verses that are pre-printed. Back when I did The Joshua Quilt, I had never really seen Bible verses printed on fabric, and so that was something that I taught myself how to do. Now it wouldn't really be a big deal. I'll just say that you need to go with whatever your inspiration is and whatever your relationship is with the Holy Spirit.

Marylee:
Can you give an example of how particular Bible verses inspired your choice of colors and fabrics?

Gail:
Well, I can. I guess I should probably give you a little bit of an explanation of how The Joshua Quilt was really created.

First of all, it was created in response to a Bible study. It was a Bible study based on the Book of Joshua. I wanted to try to be able to represent the 12 tribes of Israel in some way. In doing so I chose to use 12 squares that make a central column: it runs right down the very center of this quilt. As I began to think about the different tribes of Israel and also the entire story in the Book of Joshua, I wanted to use fabrics or colors that were symbolic of the scripture or of the story.

The Story of the Joshua Quilt

1. GOD'S PROMISE TO ABRAHAM GENESIS 22
   STAR FABRIC + SAND FABRIC

2. COURAGE JOSHUA 1:6a
   TEAL

3. OBEDIENCE JOSHUA 1:7b
   "TRUE BLUE"

4. RAHAB, THE PROSTITUTE JOSHUA 2:21b
   RED

5. QUOTE: BEST IS A LIFE IN GOD
   PURPLE

6. HOLY GROUND JOSHUA 5:15
   BROWN

7. WAR & DESTRUCTION JOSHUA 6:20
   ORANGE & BLACK

8. REASSURANCE JOSHUA 8:1a
   GREEN

9. REFUGE JOSHUA 20:9
   YELLOW & GREEN

10. QUOTE: LORD, MAKE US PARTICIPANTS IN YOUR (
    LIGHT & DARK SWIRL FABRIC

11. COMMANDMENT TO LOVE JOSHUA 23:11
    PINK

12. FREEDOM OF CHOICE JOSHUA 24:14-15
    LIGHT & DARK BLUES

For instance, the first square at the top of the quilt is one that has star fabric. Then, there's this wavy gold fabric. The fabrics were based on the promise that God made to the Israelites that they would be as numerous as the stars in the sky and the sand in the sea.

There's no printed scripture or Bible verses in that first square at the top, but for the remaining 11 squares, I chose colors that went with a Bible verse or with a certain quote from the author of the Joshua study.

The Bible Study That Inspired The Joshua Quilt

Marylee:
Gail, what prompted you to make The Joshua Quilt?

Gail:
Well, it's interesting. Sometimes somebody can ask you something or say just a few words to you, and it ends up changing your life. One day in May of 2009, I was a Bible study leader, and I was walking into a meeting with the Christian Education Director of the church.

Another Bible study leader said, "Gail, do you think that you could make something to represent the Joshua study?"

At the time I just thought, "Oh, I don't know about that." I knew why she'd asked me, and it dealt with me having made the 12-inch quilted block that I mentioned earlier, and so she knew that I could quilt.

I still don't really know whether she was asking me to make another block or if she wanted me to make a quilt. She just said, "Could you make something to represent the Joshua study?"

Marylee:
Can I just ask you—for people who don't know what The Joshua Quilt is—can you just generally say what that is?

God's Gift Within

Gail:
Well, The Joshua Quilt is a quilt that I made in response to the Presbyterian Women's Bible Study for the year 2009-2010. The study was called "Joshua: A Journey of Faith." It was written by Dr. Mary Mikhael. If you are a member of the Presbyterian Women, you will receive *Horizons* magazine, which also includes the study for that year. I didn't know anything about the study because I did not receive that magazine.

To go back to answering the question: What is The Joshua Quilt? It was my response to that study, and if you just want to get a short version of this, it's a quilt made up of 12 squares that go down a central column of the quilt. Each square is representative of the 12 tribes of Israel. In each square, there is either a Bible verse or a quote from Dr. Mary Mikhael.

On either side of this central column there are matching fabric bars, and the bars at the top begin the story of the Israelites being in captivity. The fabrics are carefully chosen to represent things like the plagues in Egypt, or the muddy Jordan River, or the land of promise flowing with milk and honey.

Once I had finished making this much of the quilt, I knew it needed to have a little something extra. I had never really tried "prairie points"—the little triangles of colored fabric that are added as decorative elements on many quilts. I decided to add prairie points between the central column and a fabric border.

It turned out that there were 70 prairie points, which correlates to the 70 elders. These were the elders who governed the Israelites. It's my interpretation of the study of Joshua. Not only just the book by Dr. Mikhael, but also what I felt when I was reading through the entire Book of Joshua.

To go back and say a little bit more about what prompted me to make this quilt, when I was asked if I could make something, at the time my mother was in her 90s. I was anticipating a move, and I really just had my hands full. I pretty much kind of said, "I don't have a copy of that study." I was trying to backpedal my way out, I guess you could say. This woman looked at me, and she said, "Oh, I have a copy of the study, and here, you can have it because my daughter's getting married, and I won't need it until sometime in the fall." This was May. Again, I don't make a quilt unless I feel led by the Holy Spirit.

I read the Bible study book, and I was fascinated by what Dr. Mary Mikhael had to say. It was a different perspective about the Middle East. She talked about things I had never thought about. I was fascinated with her personal information at the front of the study, but then the study said, "Go and read the Book of Joshua."

I read the Book of Joshua from first chapter to last. In that first chapter, it starts talking about, "Do not be discouraged. Do not be afraid," and that really struck a personal chord with me because of all of the things that were going on in my own life. I knew then that there was a quilt in this whole process, and I would end up making it. I didn't know what shape,

The Story of the Joshua Quilt

form, or fashion it would take. It would be a process, but I was going to make a quilt, so that's what prompted it.

Interpreting the Book of Joshua in Fabric

Marylee:
Would you like to share with our audience some details about the quilt and its construction?

Gail:
Absolutely. The quilt project brought to mind that a quilt can be representative of the Trinity. In making a quilt, there's three parts to the quilt; there's a top, a batting, and a backing. The top can be representative of God, the Master Creator; and the batting, which is unseen, represents the Holy Spirit. Just like the Holy Spirit, the batting provides the comfort and the warmth. The backing and binding represents Jesus Christ. He's our bond to the Holy Spirit and to God. We're incomplete without Him, just as a quilt would be incomplete.

Marylee:
Let's talk in more detail about The Joshua Quilt itself. What was your original plan going into this?

Gail:
Originally, I just thought I'm not going to spend a lot of money. I'm going to use remnants that I had, pieces of fabric leftover from previous sewing projects, and to make it representative of the Israelites. They were a remnant people, so I thought

The Story of the Joshua Quilt

the remnants would be a good representation. I was planning to make 12 squares, or 12 representations to represent the 12 tribes of Israel. Originally, each of those would be represented by a single color.

Marylee:
Did this plan evolve as you got into the project?

Gail:
Oh, yes. As I got into it, this idea would evolve into the quilt having a muslin background—as a foundation—and that I would have 13 geometric shapes of fabric sewn on to a square that was about six by six inches. Each of those squares would become more involved with scripture, or a quote from the author of the study.

Muslin foundation

Marylee:
As you got into the construction of those squares, how did the creation of this quilt change your understanding of the Book of Joshua?

Gail:
I began to do a little bit of a research to try to understand what the tribes were about, and the only background I had to go on was maybe the Native Americans' tribes. When you think about them, you would think, "Well, the Navajo would have a particular jewelry style, versus the Apache. There would be a difference in fabrics that were used by the Seminoles versus a Southwestern tribe. The Native Americans in the northwest would have had different tribal customs, or tribal fabrics, or clothing."

I thought maybe that was the way it was with the tribes of Israel, and I ended up knowing that, "No. It was more like you knew what family you belonged to." That totally made sense, because being a Southerner, you know what family you belong to. Most of the time, you are well-versed in who everybody else belongs to, and the family dog, and their whole history. That made sense and it helped me in understanding the book to kind of put it together that, no, it wasn't a particular weaving, or a particular headband, or anything like that. It was more that you knew.

Overcoming the Obstacle of a Cross-Country Move

———————&———————

Marylee:
That's really interesting. In the middle of making this quilt, which was a pretty big project, you had to set it aside and do a big move. Can you tell me what happened with that move?

Gail:
In that particular case, I was going to be moving a 90-something-year-old mother. I was moving a teenage son, and I was joining a husband who had already been in the new location for about a year. I was having to do some of the house searching online. I wasn't necessarily able to leave caregiving and go visit sites and houses, and I was having to rely on other people to provide me pictures of housing. I had a lot of balls in the air so to speak.

Marylee:
During this move which, inevitably, is chaotic and disruptive, how did you keep your quilt materials from getting lost in the midst of all the packing boxes and everything else?

Gail:
At the time that the quilt got completed, and I say "completed," but it really wasn't completed because I

had only completed the squares, but there was still a binding that had to be applied to the quilt. At that particular time, I picked up the quilted quilt from the quilter and moved the next day.

Something inside of me, a still small voice, said, "You need to put everything pertaining to this quilt in a box. You need to put the thread that matches the binding. You need to put the fabric that you're making the binding with, and everything into a box, and you need to label that box and you need to keep up with it," and I did.

Marylee:
Was that a good idea? Did you find that that helped you keep all your materials together?

Gail:
Oh yes, because otherwise, in a move, when you move, the packers put things in boxes, but they don't keep items together. If they need something to fill the top of the box, they'll just put anything in there; an extra set of towels, for instance. You may have had all your towels in the linen closet, and you thought they were all going in one box. Now you end up missing a set, because they needed something to fill the space in another box.

Marylee:
Were there any time deadlines associated with completing the quilt?

Gail:

When I was asked to make this quilt, it started out that that was in May. The study actually started in the fall, in September, and it would run through the following May. In some ways, you would have thought that if you're making something to represent the Joshua study, that you would have had it completed so that it could have been a banner displayed every time the group met, or that it would be hung in the hallway to say, as visitors came through the church, that, "Oh, this is the study we're doing, and this represents the study."

I blew all those deadlines, because the study was over and done with by the time I finished this quilt. Pretty much, I felt like a failure.

Marylee:
How did that get turned around, and who was the theological source for the aspects of the Book of Joshua that you were trying to represent?

Gail:
Let me go back and give you just a little bit of background information. Dr. Mary Mikhael was the author of the study, and she was always my theological source for the Book of Joshua. It was an interesting set of circumstances that got me really physically in touch with her.

When I took my daughter back to college in August, I drove all day long to go to Texas, and then turned around the next morning and got up and drove two and a half hours to go to church in Austin, Texas where we used to live. I had purposely brought three of the squares that I was working on for the quilt, because I wanted to show them to friends in a sewing group there at the church.

After the service was over, I met with the senior pastor and his wife, and I laid these three squares out and the pastor's wife said, "Oh, I've got to go get Aida."

I did not know Aida. She had not been a member of our sewing group, and I did not know who this person was. The pastor's wife came back and she said, "Oh, she's already gone, but you need to get in touch with her, and here's her phone number."

I took the phone number and drove back to Alabama, and the early part of that week, I ended up calling this woman, just cold turkey, and saying, "This is who I am. I got your number from the pastor's wife, and I'm working on this project and she wanted me to let you know about it."

It turned out that Aida was friends with Dr. Mary Mikhael, and so she was overjoyed with the news about the quilt and me making it. The news just thrilled her. I said, "Are you in touch with her?" She said, "Yes." I said, "Would it be possible for you to ask her some questions for me?"

She wrote them down, and there were questions about the tribes and how you would know which tribe you belonged to, and it was things like, "I'm looking for fabric for this quilt. Is the Jordan River really always the muddy Jordan?"

Examining the Quilt Square By Square

Marylee:
How did your conversations with Dr. Mikhael influence what you did when you were going to make the squares of the quilt?

Gail:
Our conversations continued, but eventually I pretty much had the answers that I felt like I needed. I began to actually work in earnest on the quilt.

For those of you who don't have a picture of the quilt in front of you, the quilt is basically 12 squares that go right down the central column, as shown on page 21. I'm going to start explaining to you a little bit in detail about these squares.

SQUARE ONE

The first square, and all the rest, are based on a foundation of muslin. This was pre-printed, and there were 13 geometric shapes. The first square has star fabric and gold, wavy fabric and 13 shapes, folded and pressed and run out to the edge of a square.

The next square starts to take on the scripture verses.

SQUARE TWO

The first scripture verse that I used begins with the first chapter of Joshua. In that chapter, it talks about, "Be strong and courageous."

When I think about courage, I think about it being a combination; you're never really alone. To find a color to represent that, I chose teal, because teal is a combination color.

When you think about having courage, there are different forms and types of courage, like a little child that's standing on a wall and the daddy is standing in front of him and holds out his arms, and the little child jumps. It takes courage for that little child to jump and have faith that dad's going to catch him. Then, you also think about courage as being somebody like Todd Beamer who, in the events of 9/11, said, "Let's roll."

When you think about Joshua and God, God reassured Joshua, "Have courage and lead the Israelites. I will never forsake you. I will never leave you." This is a message that goes continually throughout the Book of Joshua.

The Story of the Joshua Quilt

SQUARE THREE

In the next square, as we go down, it's all pale blue, and it has a Bible verse printed on it that says, "Be careful to obey all the law my servant Moses gave you. Do not turn from it to the right or the left, that you may be successful wherever you go."

I chose blue thinking of being "true blue" and being true blue in obedience to God's laws. That also is another theme throughout Joshua that the people needed to be obedient to God.

SQUARE FOUR

The fourth square is red, all different colors of red. The Bible verse that's printed on it is, "And she tied the scarlet cord to the window." This is the story of Rahab.

    Rahab gets our attention for a couple of reasons. She was a prostitute, and the spies had visited with her, and she recognized the spies as being people of God. She was told that if she wanted to save her family during the time the army would come and take the city, she should place a red cord in the window.

Her family was spared because she did that, and when I think about Rahab, I think she was despised by women then, just as prostitutes are despised by many women in this day and time, but Joshua says when the spies left, she hung that cord in the window. She didn't think about it for a day or two. She didn't hesitate. She just went and did it.

God's Gift Within

SQUARE FIVE

The next square is one that is a quote from Dr. Mary Mikhael, and this was very meaningful to me from the standpoint that having moved and lived in different parts of the country, the verse talks about rest in God. The quote goes, "Rest is a life in God where we're dwelling in the presence of God and where God participates in our lives no matter where we may find ourselves geographically."

All of the fabrics in this square are done in purple.

The Story of the Joshua Quilt

SQUARE SIX

The sixth square is brown, and it represents Joshua 5:15 which says, "Remove the sandals from your feet, for the ground where you stand is holy." The brown fabric represents the dust of the land. We often think of holy places as being temples, or sanctuaries, or cathedrals. This command was given to Joshua near the city of Jericho as he was preparing to take the city. Joshua did what he was told. He was a leader as well as a follower.

God's Gift Within

SQUARE SEVEN

The next square is a combination of orange and black, and it's based on the scripture Joshua 6:20. "When the trumpet sounded, the people shouted, and at the sound of the trumpet, when the people gave a loud shout, the wall collapsed, so every man charged straight in and they took the city."

I don't understand war. There are people who understand it, who study its strategies, know its rules. I chose to print the scripture in this particular square in a language that I did not know, that I did not understand, and I chose Hebrew. There are people who understand Hebrew, and I wish I did, but I don't. The orange fabrics represent the heat of the battle. The black represents the destruction.

God's Gift Within

SQUARE EIGHT

Green was chosen for the eighth square. It says, "The Lord said to Joshua, 'Do not be afraid. Do not be discouraged.' " God was reassuring Joshua one more time. To me, this is the piece of the 23rd Psalm which says, "Even though I walk through the valley of the shadow of death, I will fear no evil, for you are with me."

SQUARE NINE

The next square, the 9th square, is a square that has green fabrics on the outer edges, and in the center portions, there's yellow. The yellow fabrics have stars, flowers, and bees. The verse that's printed there is from Joshua 20:9, and it says, "Any of the Israelites, or any alien living among them who killed someone accidentally could flee to these designated cities and not be killed by the avenger of blood prior to standing trial before the assembly." The yellow fabric with the stars, flowers, and bees would represent the freedom that these refugees might find.

God's Gift Within

SQUARE TEN

This next square has a quote from Dr. Mary Mikhael, "Lord, make us participants in your grace." The fabrics are a light and a dark, both full of designs. The lighter fabric has dots and swirls. The darker fabric has rainbow colors. Again, lots of swirl to them. These fabrics were chosen to represent the complexity of all that goes on in our universe.

Dr. Mikhael stated in her study, this is her response to every time she sees a rainbow, "Lord, make us participants in your grace." Every time you

see this rainbow, you should think about your stewardship of your time on earth.

This also, in the study, represented the covenant that God had made with Noah and the undeserved favor—God's promise that he would never destroy the earth again. "Lord, make us participants in your undeserved favor."

SQUARE ELEVEN

The next to the last square is pink, and it's all kinds of pinks. It's very soft pinks with polka dots; it's checkered pinks; it's rosy pinks; it's pink with flowers. The Bible verse is from Joshua 23:11, "So be very careful to love the Lord your God."

As I thought about that, I understood that the verse is a commandment. Does anybody really have to tell you, Be careful to love your grandchildren? No. But, the verse was a commandment. The verse commands us to be deliberate in loving God. If you love someone, you want to spend time with them. Are you spending time with God? Are you drinking a cup of coffee with Him?

The Story of the Joshua Quilt

SQUARE TWELVE

The last square is light and dark blues. The light blue is really white with a light blue design, and the font that was chosen for the scripture verse is very hard to read, and then the darks are very dark. There's a big contrast in this particular square, and it's a contrast to represent two different forms of worship in the final square.

The quote comes from Joshua 24:14-15.

"Now fear the LORD and serve him with all faithfulness. Throw away the gods your forefathers worshiped beyond the River and in

Egypt, and serve the LORD. But if serving the LORD seems undesirable to you, then choose for yourselves this day whom you will serve, whether the gods your forefathers served beyond the River, or the gods of the Amorites, in whose land you are living. But as for me and my household, we will serve the LORD."

Standing Back From the Quilt

Marylee:
Can you tell us more about what the specific squares represent and what fabrics you chose for them?

Gail:
The top fabric is a really dark, black fabric and it represents the Israelites being captured.

The next, or second, bar of fabric is a lighter dark fabric, so there's brown mixed into it. It's a Batik fabric, but there's still a lot of black, so it's still continuing their journey in that they are in captivity.

On either side of the central column of squares are horizontal bars of fabric. Those borders continue on the left- and right-hand sides of the squares, and they go all the way to the bottom of the quilt.

The third bar is one of frogs. It's a light colored fabric and there are red frogs, green frogs, yellow frogs, and blue frogs. This represents the plagues of Egypt. The Israelites were in Egypt before they were released from their captivity.

The fourth fabric is a very light tan, beige fabric with tiny black dots all over it, and if you're standing a distance away from it, you just hardly see those dots at all, but it represents the multitude of the Israelites who were living in the desert.

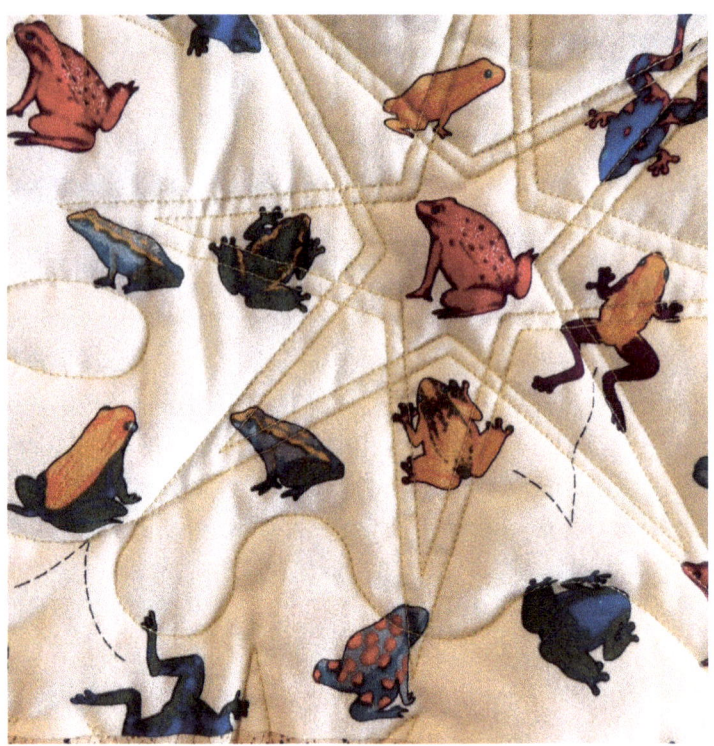

Frogs represent the plagues of Egypt.

    The next fabric is a muddy, frothy fabric, and I think actually when I bought it, it probably had something to do with coffee, but in this quilt it actually represents the muddy Jordan river.

    The next fabric is also a brown fabric, but a different color brown than the muddy Jordan. This band has white dots on it, and they're not round dots. They're kind of an oval shaped, and these ovals represent the stones of Gilgal. Once the Israelites crossed the muddy Jordan, they built an altar there.

The next fabric is a green background fabric, and it has brown dots on it. It's similar to the one that represents the Israelites wandering the desert; but in this case, the background fabric is green. Some of the dots are a little bit larger and some a little bit smaller; the pattern represents them moving into their new land.

Then the last five fabrics are alternating. They represent the land flowing with milk and honey. The milk is a fabric that is very white, and two of the white bars represent the milk. The bar in the middle is representative of honey because it's got honeybees on it. The top and bottom bars are a flowing, vine fabric.

That represents their journey from captivity to freedom in the land of promise.

When I finished the squares in the center column, the quilt was very narrow, and I said, "Well, it needs a border to make it wider." I went ahead and put a border that was the same color as representing the Israelites wandering in the desert.

God's Gift Within

Prairie Points Represent the 70 Elders

Marylee:
When did you add the prairie points?

Gail:
After I'd sewn the border on both sides, I thought, it just really does not look right. It was missing something, and so I decided to make prairie points to set off the main body of the quilt from the border.

I didn't do the math to figure out how many points I'd need. I just picked a size square and I started cutting fabric. When you make a prairie point, you take a square of fabric, and you fold it so that it becomes triangular. Then you sew the raw edges, which are all to one side, into the seam.

I just began to make these prairie points, and as I was doing them, I kept thinking wouldn't it be neat if 70 prairie points fit onto the sides of this so that it would be representative of the 70 elders who governed the Israelites. As you may well guess, that's exactly what happened, and I didn't even use a ruler to space them apart. It's just that's the way it worked out.

A lot of the prairie points are the fabrics that were used in the squares in this central column. On purpose I turned one fabric wrong side out, and I did

The Story of the Joshua Quilt

so to represent that sometimes you get turned wrong side out in your thinking, and hopefully you are in association with other people who can turn your thinking around and get you pointed in the right direction.

The other thing that happened, in this use of prairie points, is that I have one green prairie point that decided it was not going to point in the direction that it was intended to point. It is flipped backwards in the other direction. No matter what I did—other than if I were to take needle and thread and stitch it down—that prairie point would not stay in place.

I've decided that this prairie point is like people we associate with, and sometimes, they are going in the opposite direction, whether it's the wrong direction or just opposite from the direction we're going.

When I got to the point that this quilt was going to be quilted, I took it in to a quilt shop and talked with a lady who would quilt it. I told her that I wanted this quilt to puff. My mother's hand-quilted quilts always puffed. There's a different feel to a hand-quilted quilt than to one that's machine-quilted because a lot of times machine-quilted quilts have a flat appearance.

The woman chose the batting that would be put into The Joshua Quilt. I told her the only thing I really cared about was that I wanted there to be a star pattern throughout the quilt and that I wanted it to be stitched with yellow quilting thread. I left the rest up to her.

The way that the quilt is constructed, there's the center portion and then the row of prairie points on either side, and then the border. In the border area, she took the time to make the stars more dense —closer together. In the main body the stars are a bigger pattern.

Meeting The Theologian

Marylee:
Once you finished this quilt, did you ever have a chance to meet with the theologian who'd come up with the idea for the Joshua study, Dr. Mary Mikhael?

Gail:
This is an interesting question. Just prior to one of our moves, we had had a member of our church in Austin pass away, and I had not written a check in his memory. In the meantime, we moved. It was along toward August or first part of September when I finally got my wits about me and said, "Oh yes, you never wrote that check."

I wrote the check, got ready to address the envelope, and I could not remember the address for the church. I knew exactly where it was in Austin, but I had to go Google it and get the address. While I was on the church's website, the newsletter came up on the screen, and I said, "Well, while I'm here, I might as well just read what's going on in the church."

As I scrolled down, I saw this picture of Dr. Mikhael. She was going to be at the church in about two and a half weeks. She would give talks there on Sunday morning, Sunday afternoon, and Sunday evening. It dawned on me that sometime back when I had been talking to her and e-mailing back and forth, she said she had a desire to meet with me and to see this quilt, and my response had been, "I don't travel out of the country."

I'll remind you that she was living in Beirut, Lebanon. She was the President of the Near East Theological Seminary there, and so this was a huge opportunity. She would be in the States, she would be in a city that I was familiar with, and in a church that I was familiar with.

It turned out that that evening at dinner I told my husband, "Guess who is going to be in Austin?" He had no idea what I was talking about, and so I told him and he said, "Oh, okay."

Then a little while later, our son came in, and I said, "Guess who's going to be in Austin?"

"Who?" he said.

I told him, and at this point in time, my husband kind of perked up and said, "Would you really like to go hear her?"

I was like, "Oh, yes. This is probably the only opportunity I will ever be able to be that close to her and get to visit with her, and I want her to see this quilt."

Then you have to go back to that box that had the quilt in it, the binding in it, the thread in it because that box held a quilt that wasn't finished yet.

By this time, things had changed. I didn't have a sewing room to spread the quilt out in, I didn't have a room hardly big enough to set my sewing machine up in, but I knew where that sewing machine was, I knew where that box was that held that quilt, and in two weeks' time, I would have that quilt finished. It would be completely bound.

We went about getting the preparations for the trip. I made an airline reservation, and I called our daughter; she was living in Texas at the time. She was going to meet me and pick me up, but it turned out that the day that I flew, the airlines lost my luggage. Fortunately, I had put everything into my checked luggage except the quilt, and I had hand-carried that on.

Here I was set to meet this person that I had taken the liberty to create a quilt using her material,

Aida, Dr. Mikhael, and Gail discussing the quilt.

and I didn't have a change of clothes, I didn't have a toothbrush, I didn't have really anything. I ended up picking up some clothes, picking up toiletries, and getting myself put together, and I made it to meet Dr. Mikhael.

At that meeting was the senior pastor of the church and his wife and Aida and Dr. Mikhael and our daughter and myself. I will just say that it was quite an emotional meeting and that Dr. Mikhael, after I had explained to her what everything was in the quilt and the representation of the fabrics and everything, she looked at me and she said, "This needs to be in a museum."

Again, my response to her was, "Oh, but a museum! I want people to see it." Well, where else would you see it, but in a museum? And then it registered with me that all I had ever wanted to do really was to be an artist, and artists have their work in museums.

The quilt is not in a museum at this point in time, and it has never actually been displayed in a museum. It has been displayed as an art project, but that was in a private residence. I'm still looking for that museum experience.

How The Worlds of Quilting and Bible Study Have Changed

Marylee:
Well, it's obvious you've become a very creative and brave person through this combination of quilting and Bible study. How is the world of quilting and Bible study different now than when you got started?

Gail:
Well, the world of quilting is completely different, because if you take it back to when my mom got started, it was cutting things by hand. It was tracing patterns on newspaper.

As I moved through and worked with my mom, I graduated to a rotary cutter and a mat board and the use of acrylic templates; but this day and time, they have a system that is similar to a Sizzix machine where you have a die cut, and you lay fabric on top of it, and you roll that through a machine, similar to a mimeograph. It's a two-roller machine, and it cuts pieces of fabric into whatever die cut you had laying underneath them.

This assures you of accuracy in your cuts and also of not having to have the hand-eye coordination that is necessary with a pair of scissors or the dexterity that's necessary to use a rotary cutter.

Quilting has changed quite a bit. Now, quilters have the ability to design a quilt digitally on a computer. It's not difficult. You pick and choose pieces, and you can figure out what color combinations you want to use, and you can have the design right before your very eyes on a computer.

 I guess Bible study in some ways has remained the same in that people gather in groups and read the Bible together and study it. I don't see as many changes with Bible study as I do with quilting.

Disruptive Events Turn Out To Be God's Greatest Gifts

Marylee:
How has your creation of the quilt led you to think about how the most disruptive events in our lives can also turn out to be our greatest gifts?

Gail:
Well, this kind of goes back to our move to Tuscaloosa. When we moved, it was a difficult move. We were, again, transporting at that point in time two children with us, plus my mom, and we had separate vehicles to move. We were a caravan moving from Texas to Alabama, and it was just difficult.

When we got there, we realized there was just a tremendous amount of damage to our goods and furniture. We got there middle of the week on a Wednesday, and by Saturday, I had just kind of had it. You know that saying about "when the going gets tough, the tough go shopping" kind of thing?

Well, I just decided I've had enough, and so our daughter and I decided that we would go to the mall. We really had nothing that we were going there to buy. We were just going to see what was at the mall and to create a diversion from everything that was going on at the house.

When we got there, we went into Dillard's

God's Gift Within

Barbie shoes and Jesus sandals

department store, and they were having a sale. They had all these folding tables lined up right at the edge of the shoe department. They had shoes in boxes, and the majority of these shoes were $5 a pair. Just on a lark, I decided to step out of what I call my "Jesus sandals." These were Mephisto sandals that were well-worn. I stepped into a pair of what I refer to as "Barbie shoes."

The Barbie shoes would take me across the department store to the other side. These Barbie shoes were truly just like what Barbie would wear. Strap across your toes, no strap behind your heels, probably about one and a half inches of heel, and two-toned green. I got across the store and heard a woman say, "Whose shoes are these?"

I realized that they were my shoes. I didn't really want to go across there to meet this woman.

There was nothing wrong with her. She was nicely dressed; she was a pleasant person. She was just really curious about my shoes, but based on what I had been through, I was just like, I guess, afraid to go over and meet her.

But I realized that she wasn't going anywhere. You could say that she was somewhat homesteading by my shoes, and so I thought, "Okay, there is no way I'm going to get my shoes back unless I go over there."

I went over there and said hello. She looked at me and said, "These your shoes?" and I was like, "Yeah?" and I rolled my eyes at her. She goes, "You just moved here, didn't you, honey?" I said, "Yeah, I did," and I'm looking at this like, "How in the world did she know that?"

"I moved here about a year ago," she said. "It gets better." She continued to ask me about the shoes, and I told her that they were from Austin, Texas, and she said, "I knew they weren't from around here." Turned out, she'd been looking for shoes like mine.

We continued to stand there and talk, and the conversation ended up, "Did I have a church to go to?" I said, "Well, I visited some churches," and she wanted to know which ones, and I told her, and then she said, "Well, I go to First Presbyterian." And then she said, "I'd really like to have you come and join me in the morning at 8:15 at the early service."

She started searching in her purse, and I couldn't help but think, "What is she doing?" She pulled out her checkbook and tore off her name, address, and phone number from a deposit slip. She gave it to me and said, "Make sure you call me and let me know if you're going to come so that I can be standing outside waiting for you."

I ended up walking away from there with a pair of Barbie shoes, and I have those Barbie shoes still today, and I still have those Jesus sandals, and I ended up calling and saying, "I'll meet you outside in the morning at 8:15."

That move was probably one of the most disruptive events in my life, and yet the gift of meeting this woman in this store was probably one of my life's greatest gifts.

Marylee:
Are you still friends with her today?

Gail:
We are. We are still friends with each other to this day. Keep up with each other on Facebook, talk to each other, concerned about what goes on in each other's lives, and actually when we moved to Arizona, she put me in touch with one of her friends that lives in Arizona and so again, she's continued to work in my life.

Marylee:
Definitely a gift.

Gail:
Oh, yeah.

How Readers Can Discover Their Own Gifts

Marylee:
Let's switch gears a little bit now and move into the present where our audience of women of faith, quilters, Bible study groups, storytellers, caregivers, and quilt museum curators want to get started on this unique journey to discover their own gifts. I'm going to ask you a series of questions about what you would do if you had to start all over again right now from scratch.

You've had life events that seem to be a part of many people's lives: frequent job moves, caring for relatives, and raising children. Yet, these events also deepened your faith and gave you insight into how to handle stress. If you had to start all over again with this ever busier world we live in, what would you do differently?

Gail:
Well, I always wanted to be an artist. I wanted to go to New York and study art, but my parents would never allow that. There was always the question with them, "Can you make a living at doing this?"

If I had it to do over, I would've pursued that career in art or the study of art. It wouldn't have necessarily had to have been in New York City.

Marylee:
What would you do less of?

Gail:
I'd worry less about the dust in the house and the grit on the floor.

Marylee:
Even in Texas?

Gail:
Even in Texas.

Marylee:
What about faster? Is there anything faster that you would have done?

Gail:
Not really anything faster. I just wish I had realized a long time ago that God's timing is perfect.

Marylee:
Where should women of faith, quilters, Bible study groups, storytellers, caregivers, and quilt museum curators focus their efforts if they want to succeed with what life throws at them?

Gail:
I think this is my thoughts whether you're a quilt curator or just any person really. You need to have a relationship with your Father God, and when I say relationship, I really mean you spend time talking to God and you spend time listening for His response.

Marylee:
Do you see Bible study and quilting as a way to discover joy and contentment even in the midst of stress?

Gail:
Oh, yes. I remember when I was working on The Joshua Quilt, a lot of the times, I was busy all during the day and I didn't have time to just take a day and devote to just working on that project. A lot of times it was when all the chores were done. Maybe most of the family was already in bed and I would work on this at night, and it gave me something different to think about. It gave me a different set of problems to solve, so to speak.

Often when I was doing that, I was either praying, "God, give me the inspiration to know what to do next with this," or I was humming a hymn while I was trying to figure out what the next step was.

Marylee:
Where do you see the overlooked opportunities in quilting and Bible study right now? What about unopened gifts?

Gail:
Well, I've been involved in quilting and sewing groups at churches, and I've been involved in Bible studies, but I have never had the two together at the same time.

Quilting and Time Management
———————————&———————————

Marylee:
What are the best quilting and Bible study tools ordinary people struggling with unexpected events in their lives need to know about and use?

Gail:
When you're doing quilting, buy the best that you can afford. Whether it's the best quilting thread or the best quilting fabric, buy the very best that you can afford and use it.

Then, if you're looking at when you go to do a batting, you've got to think about who's the person that's going to use this. Are they living in a warm climate? Are they living in a cold climate they could benefit from a quilt with a wool batting?

Then you have to think about is this quilt going to be hand quilted or is it going to be machine quilted. The quilt's thickness makes a difference in the needle piercing through two fabrics and a batting. Check out the local quilt store or the person that's going to be actually doing your quilting because they may have a personal preference, or there may be something new on the market. You wouldn't know about it without seeking out that person's expertise or that expertise in the store.

Marylee:
Do you have any tips for time management when it comes to quilting?

Gail:
Well, as a caregiver, you have to learn to be flexible. You can have all the best laid plans, and then the unexpected happens. With my mom, for instance, she would be fine and I'd be ready to get out the door, and then she would just turn sick or her heart would start fluttering, and you cannot leave.

You end up giving up a lot. I ended up coming to look at these instances as "they happened for a reason." I also came to accept the fact that God wasn't necessarily sharing what the reason was. I just realized and knew that my mom needed me more than I needed to be somewhere else, and I also recognized that this was not going to last forever.

Overcoming Obstacles

———————— & ————————

Marylee:
Caregiving is a common situation people confront today. Do you think it's easier or harder for an ordinary person struggling with the curves life throws at them then it was for you when you were in the thick of it?

Gail:
Well, I think now there is much more awareness of caregivers. There are also many more hospice entities and information resources.

Marylee:
How would you sum up everything we've discussed today in a few final thoughts? Do you have some advice for all of our listeners?

Gail:
I'd like to share a quote from the movie, *Chariots of Fire*, and it's Eric Liddell. He's talking about people who've come to see the race he won that day, and he says:
> "You came to see a race today, to see someone win, and it happened to be me, but I want you to do more than just watch a race. I want you to take part in it. I want to compare faith to running in a race. It's hard. It requires concentration of

will, energy of soul. You experience elation when the winner breaks the tape, especially if you've got a bet on it, but how long does that last? You go home. Maybe your dinner's burnt. Maybe you haven't got a job.

"So who am I to say believe, have faith in the face of life's realities. I would like to give you something more permanent, but I can only point the way. I have no formula for winning the race. Everyone runs in her own way or his own way, and where does the power come from to see the race to its end. From within. Jesus said, 'Behold, the kingdom of God is within you. If with all your heart you truly seek me, you shall ever surely find me.' If you commit yourself to the love of Christ, then that is how you run a straight race."

Marylee:
What about you, Gail? How do these gifts apply to you?

Gail:
I want to go back and talk about my mom for a minute.

During the time that I was making The Joshua Quilt, I found out that I was an unplanned event in my parents' lives, and my mom never elaborated on it. It was just kind of a simple, one-sentence statement that she made one day and we never, ever talked about it again.

When God gave her the gift of a second child, I was a normal child, and at the time that she found out that she was going to have me, I'm sure she had a

God's Gift Within

Mother and daughter

lot of worries, a lot of concerns, a lot of misgivings. My older brother was mentally retarded, both my parents worked, and now they were going to add to their family.

In the end, this second-born child would maintain a relationship with her brother until the day he died, she would help with decision making as her father succumbed to Alzheimer's, and she would take her mother in to live with her for more than a decade.

I never thought of myself as being a gift, but that one simple statement brought me back to thinking about children as a gift from God. It's talked about in the 127th Psalm, and I know that I was a gift to my mom.

Then when I think about the other gifts—the gift of talent—of me being able to sew and to design and to create, these gifts were in my life all along. It was just a matter of opening them up and using them. It was a matter of putting aside uncomfortableness and fear. It meant listening to the Holy Spirit and following that still, small voice that was working inside of heart and head.

When fully opened, it wasn't just one gift, but it was many. It was the gift of friendship and sisterhood from the sewing circle group. It was a textile creation recognizing Scripture that was written centuries ago being relevant in today's world. It was the mystery of God bringing people from around the world together.

It was a gift to share and inspire.

Marylee:
Thank you very much, Gail. Terrific and inspiring interview.

Gail:
Thank you.

&

God's Gift Within

About Marylee MacDonald

———————— ————————

Interviewer Marylee MacDonald helps aspiring authors write their books. She is the author of two books: *Montpelier Tomorrow* and *Bonds of Love & Blood*.
Follow her blog about writing, publishing and marketing books.
www.maryleemacdonaldauthor.com

She also blogs about issues affecting caregivers.
www.maryleemacdonald.org

Connect with her on Twitter @MaryleeMacD
Or on Facebook: MaryleeMacD

Contact Gail Howard Gibson

Gail Howard Gibson is an expert in quilting and Bible study whose accomplishments include a B.S. in Home Economics, Berry College and an M.S. in Consumer Affairs, Auburn University. On the personal front, she has been a "domestic engineer," specializing in moving and raising two children. Also, she was an in-home caregiver for her mother for fourteen years.

Gail Howard Gibson started sewing and quilting with her mother, grandmother, and aunts, and continued in college as a Home Economics major, and later, as a 4-H Coordinator. A longtime member of sewing and quilting groups, she has been a quilter for fifty years.

Along with her quilting history, she has designed spiritual banners, mentored confirmation classes, and been a keynote speaker at luncheons and retreats.

Quilting and Bible study expert Gail Howard Gibson is both an ordinary person and uniquely qualified to help you understand everything you need to know about how God orchestrates the details in our lives. With God's help, she stepped outside her comfort zone and made the Joshua quilt, a work of art based on scripture from the Book of Joshua.

If you'd like Gail Howard Gibson to speak at an event, please contact her at thejoshuaquilt@gmail.com.
She is on Facebook at Gail Howard Gibson
Her website is www.thejoshuaquilt.com.

www.ingramcontent.com/pod-product-compliance
Lightning Source LLC
LaVergne TN
LVHW010317070426
835507LV00026B/3433